MW00988548

ISBN 0-86163-484-5

First published in Great Britain by
Macdonald & Co (Publishers) Ltd.

The edition first published 1991 by
Award Publications Limited, 1st Floor,
Goodyear House, 52-56 Osnaburgh Street,
London, NW1 3NS

4th impression 1994

Printed in Singapore

THE DAY OF THE DINOSAURS

Written by
JOHN STIDWORTHY
MA Cantab
Consultant Editor
STEVE PARKER
BSc Zoology
Illustrated by
CHRIS FORSEY

AWARD PUBLICATIONS

4,500 million
600 million
225 million
65 milli
FIRST LIFE
PALEOZOIC
MESOZOIC
THE AGE OF REPTILES
YEARS AGO
PERMIAN
TRIASSIC
JURASSIC
280 million
225 million
195 million
136 milli

Today

CENOZOIC

CRETACEOUS

65 million

CONTENTS

REPTILES RULE THE EARTH

During the Permian period, from 280 million to 225 million years ago, the reptiles gradually took over the world. The very first reptiles lived long before this time, but they were scarce animals in a world dominated by large amphibians.

By 280 million years ago the amphibians were becoming less common and the reptiles had evolved into many types and sizes, all with different ways of life. Some were small and lizard-like – though the true lizards came along later. Others were large and clumsy. Some were plant-eaters with tough, broad teeth that could crush the Permian vegetation. A few even evolved sails on their backs, which may have helped them to control their body temperature (see page 8).

The earliest reptiles probably lived partly in the water. As time went on they were able to leave the water completely and live on the land. Most of these new land-dwellers had heavy limbs which stuck out sideways from their bodies. They had solid skulls and small brains. They laid eggs with shells, that didn't have to hatch in water. They had mastered the basics of living on land, but they must have been clumsy and slow compared to the more advanced reptiles that came later.

As the reptiles prospered, the amphibians declined. By the end of the Permian the Age of Reptiles was well under way – a reign that was to last for another 160 million years.

How to say...

Araeoscelis
Air-ee-owe-skell-is

Captorhinus
Cap-tow-rine-us

Pareiasaurus
Par-rye-ah-sore-us

Edaphosaurus
Edd-aff-owe-sore-us

Dimetrodon
Di-met-trow-don

Leaving the water

As the Permian period passed, many new reptile species appeared and rapidly took the place of the amphibians. Yet many of these new reptiles looked very similar to the amphibians they were replacing. So what made them better?

The answer seems to be that their lives had become completely independent of the water. Several adaptations helped the reptiles to do this, like having a dry, scaly skin which does not let water escape from the body. Most amphibians have a smooth, slimy skin, which allows water to evaporate quite quickly. So amphibians had to stay near water or damp places, to keep their skins moist – otherwise they would dry out. Reptiles, on the other hand, could move about on the land and didn't need to stay near to the water.

One of the most important advances made by the reptiles was in the eggs they laid. Amphibians had jelly-coated eggs – like frogs' spawn – which they had to lay in water. The eggs hatched into tadpoles, which had to live in water as well. (Today's amphibians do just the same.) The tadpoles had to grow up and change into adults before they could crawl onto dry land.

The reptiles evolved an egg with a tough, waterproof shell. It could be laid anywhere – even in a desert. The young reptile had its own 'private pond' of water inside the shell, and a good supply of food in the form of *yolk*. The young reptile hatched out as a miniature version of its parents. The shelled egg set the reptiles free to become full-time land animals.

We know that these changes happened and how important they were, but skins, eggs and tadpoles are not often fossilized. We cannot usually directly say whether a certain fossil was amphibian or reptile. Instead we have to rely on features in the skeleton to distinguish between them.

Creature-catcher
Sauroctonus *was a primitive reptile from 250 million years ago. It grew to 3 metres long and its teeth were big and sharp – a sure sign that it was a meat-eater.*

The Dawn of the Age of Reptiles

1 Araeoscelis *was a lizard-like reptile about 30 cms in length. It probably fed on insects.*

2 Captorhinus *(30 cms long) was an early reptile from 300 million years ago. It had a heavy, solid skull and a clumsy body design, similar to its amphibian ancestors.*

3 Pareiasaurus *was one of the first plant-eating reptiles.*

4 Edaphosaurus *(3 metres in length), like its cousin* Dimetrodon, *had a sail on its back. Its blunt teeth tell us it ate plants – or perhaps shellfish.*

5 Dimetrodon *was a fierce meat-eater. Its fossils are very common in rocks from about 260 million years ago, as you can read on page 8.*

Amphibian or reptile?

Many of the differences between amphibians and reptiles are shown in the soft parts of their bodies – which aren't usually preserved as fossils. However, there are also some differences in their bones, which *are* preserved. These differences give us the clues we need to work out how amphibians gradually gave way to reptiles during the Permian. For example, in a reptile's spine two bones are joined to the hip bone. But in an amphibian's spine, only one bone is joined to the hip bone. There is also a difference in the bones of the hands and feet, as you can see on the left.

Most reptiles have five 'fingers' on their hands and feet. And some fingers are made up of five or even six bones.

Many fossil amphibians, like their relatives today, have four 'fingers' or fewer on their hands and feet. Each finger is made up of only three or four bones.

Plant-crusher
Bradysaurus *was a slow-moving, plant-eating reptile of the middle Permian, that grew to 3 metres long. Its teeth were big and broad for crushing land vegetation.*

The first reptile?

One of the earliest reptiles yet discovered is *Hylonomus*, from over 300 million years ago. In 1852 many *Hylonomus* fossils were found in Nova Scotia in eastern Canada. The animals seem to have died curled up hidden in tree stumps, perhaps sheltering from a flood or other danger.

Many different types of reptiles appear in the fossil record soon after *Hylonomus*. It is unlikely that this creature was the ancestor of all of them. It was an early reptile – but probably not the first.

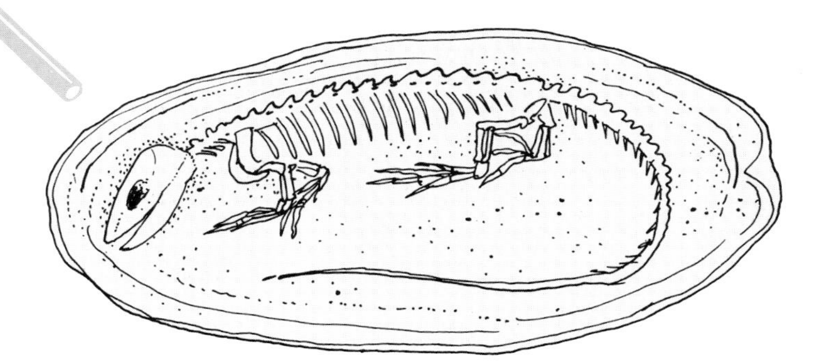

Sails in the sunrise

Some of the most interesting early reptiles belonged to a group called pelycosaurs. These can be thought of as very remote ancestors of humans, because they were on the side of the reptile 'family tree' that eventually led to the mammals (page 12).

The 'mammal-like' reptiles can be recognised by the single opening they have in the bones forming the side of the skull. Large numbers of fossilized pelycosaurs have been found in Texas, in rocks about 260 million years old. Some of these are very well preserved complete skeletons. Less complete remains are found in other parts of North America and Europe. The oldest pelycosaurs were mostly about a metre long, but they soon evolved to be 3 metres or more in length.

Some pelycosaurs were plant-eaters. They had flattened teeth, bulky bodies and small heads. *Cotylorhynchus* was one of the largest. The others were meat-eaters, and they had slim bodies, large heads and pointed teeth. *Dimetrodon* is one of the best known. It is the commonest fossil reptile found in the rocks from the early Permian period in Texas. Perhaps the most extraordinary thing about *Dimetrodon* was the enormous sail that ran down its back. This was made of skin supported by long spikes – each of which came from one bone in the spine. (The plant-eating pelycosaur *Edaphosaurus*, shown on page 5, had a similar sail.)

The most likely explanation for the sail is that it was an early attempt by reptiles to control their body temperature more effectively. A reptile's body works slowly and produces little heat. It depends on its surroundings for warmth, and in particular on heat from

All extras included!

Dimetrodon was one of the most advanced reptiles of its time, but it was not on the main line of reptile evolution. The dinosaurs and other great reptiles evolved from a separate group, the thecodonts (see page 13). *Dimetrodon* was able to warm up quickly in the morning with the help of its large, heat-absorbing sail. Other reptiles, still sluggish from the cold of the night, would be easy meat at this time of day.

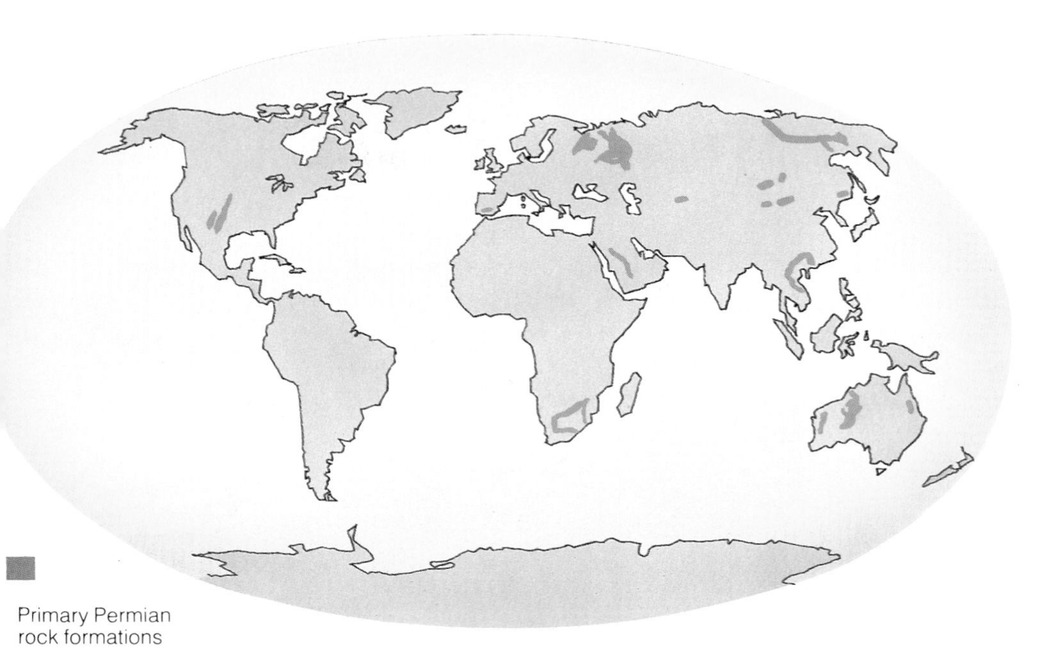

From Perm to Texas
The Permian period was named in 1841 by the Scottish geologist Roderick Murchison, after rocks found in the Perm region of the USSR. However much of today's knowledge about life during the Permian comes from the fossils such as Dimetrodon *which were found in the USA, mainly in Texas and other southern states*

the Sun. Reptiles bask in the sun to get warmer and more active, or retreat into the shade if they are too hot.

A pelycosaur could sit sideways to the Sun in the early morning and soak up the warming rays, becoming active very quickly. In the heat of the day it could cool down by lying in the shade or sitting head-on to the Sun, so that only a little area of its body and sail was exposed. But by the middle of the Permian period the pelycosaurs themselves were disappearing, to be replaced by the therapsids (page 13).

No-frills pelycosaur
Varanosaurus *was a streamlined lizard-like pelycosaur about 1 metre long. Its fossils have been found in the Permian rocks of Texas.*

RADIATING REPTILES

In the relatively brief period called the Triassic, which lasted from 225 to 195 million years ago, there were rapid changes in reptile life. Many different types of reptile evolved or 'radiated' from the species previously alive in the Permian. Early in the Triassic the plant-eating dicynodonts flourished. Oddly, these reptiles were similar to the early mammals. They had two distinctive small tusks in the upper jaw, although many of them had no other teeth. Some were no bigger than a cat, while others were over 2 metres long. Their meat-eating cousins the cynognaths flourished early on but disappeared well before the end of the period.

The place of the cynognaths was taken by the first members of an up-and-coming group of reptiles known as archosaurs – the 'ruling reptiles'. The dinosaurs belonged to this group. However the first archosaurs were not dinosaurs, but reptiles called thecodonts.

Some thecodonts were shaped like clumsy crocodiles; others were slim, lightly-built and probably quite agile. Thecodonts such as *Euparkeria* could bring their legs under their bodies, instead of having legs sticking out at the side like the earlier reptiles. This seems to be the start of the successful body design found in their descendants, the dinosaurs.

By the end of the Triassic, the first true dinosaurs roamed the world. Soon they were evolving into every way of life imaginable. The dinosaur group of reptiles was about to dominate the land while other reptiles took to the sea and air.

Reptile evolution

300 million years ago

This is an evolutionary tree showing the main groups of reptiles and their relatives. The first thing to notice is that not all the great reptiles were dinosaurs. The name dinosaur means 'terrible lizard' and was invented by Sir Richard Owen, the famous palaentologist, in 1841. But it is no longer an exact scientific term – it's now used more as a general name for any big, extinct land reptile.

The second thing to notice is that the reptiles' tree is not a neat one. It doesn't have all the extinct reptiles together in one group, leading to a single group of living reptiles. The living reptiles have evolved from different extinct reptiles. Two other very large groups – the mammals and the birds – are descended from separate lines of reptiles.

Thirdly, you can see that in the early stages of reptile evolution we aren't quite sure who is related to who. The thecodonts gave rise to many groups of reptiles, and also the birds, but exactly how this happened is not known. For the time being, until more fossils are discovered and the picture becomes clearer, scientists find it better to be fairly vague when they draw a tree like this – rather than try and be too accurate, and get it wrong!

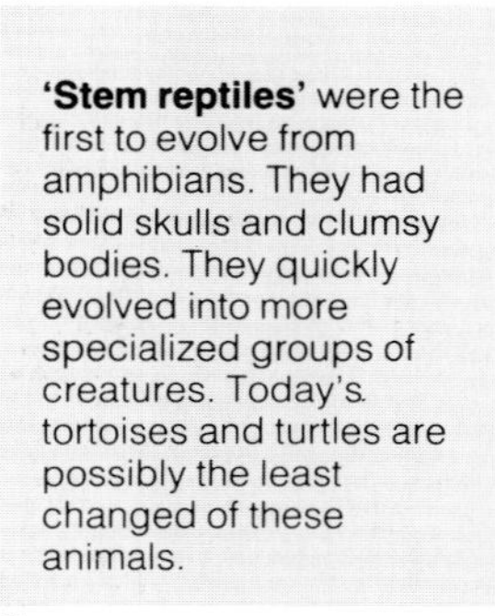

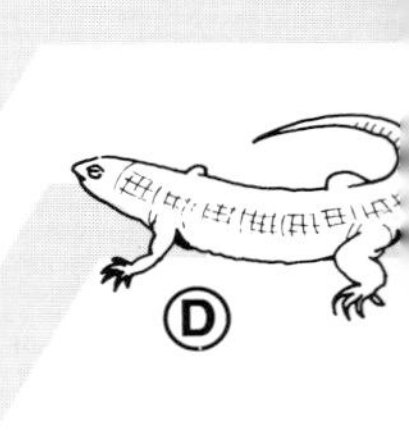

'Stem reptiles' were the first to evolve from amphibians. They had solid skulls and clumsy bodies. They quickly evolved into more specialized groups of creatures. Today's tortoises and turtles are possibly the least changed of these animals.

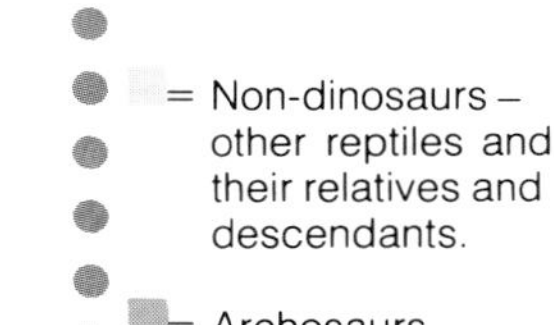

= Non-dinosaurs – other reptiles and their relatives and descendants.

= Archosaurs ('dinosaurs') – and their relatives and descendants.

Reptiles of the Triassic

1 Lystrosaurus *belonged to the reptile group known as dicynodonts. It was a tubby vegetarian and probably lived like the hippo does today, chomping water plants with its beak-like jaws.*

2 Euparkeria *was an agile reptile less than 1 metre long. It was a thecodont and could run well on all fours or on its back legs.*

3 Coelophysis *was one of the first dinosaurs. It may have used its long 'fingers' to grab its prey of small animals.*

4 Paradepedon *(2 metres in length), was a member of the herbivorous rhynchosaur group.*

5 Plateosaurus *was the first big dinosaur – growing to 8 metres long.*

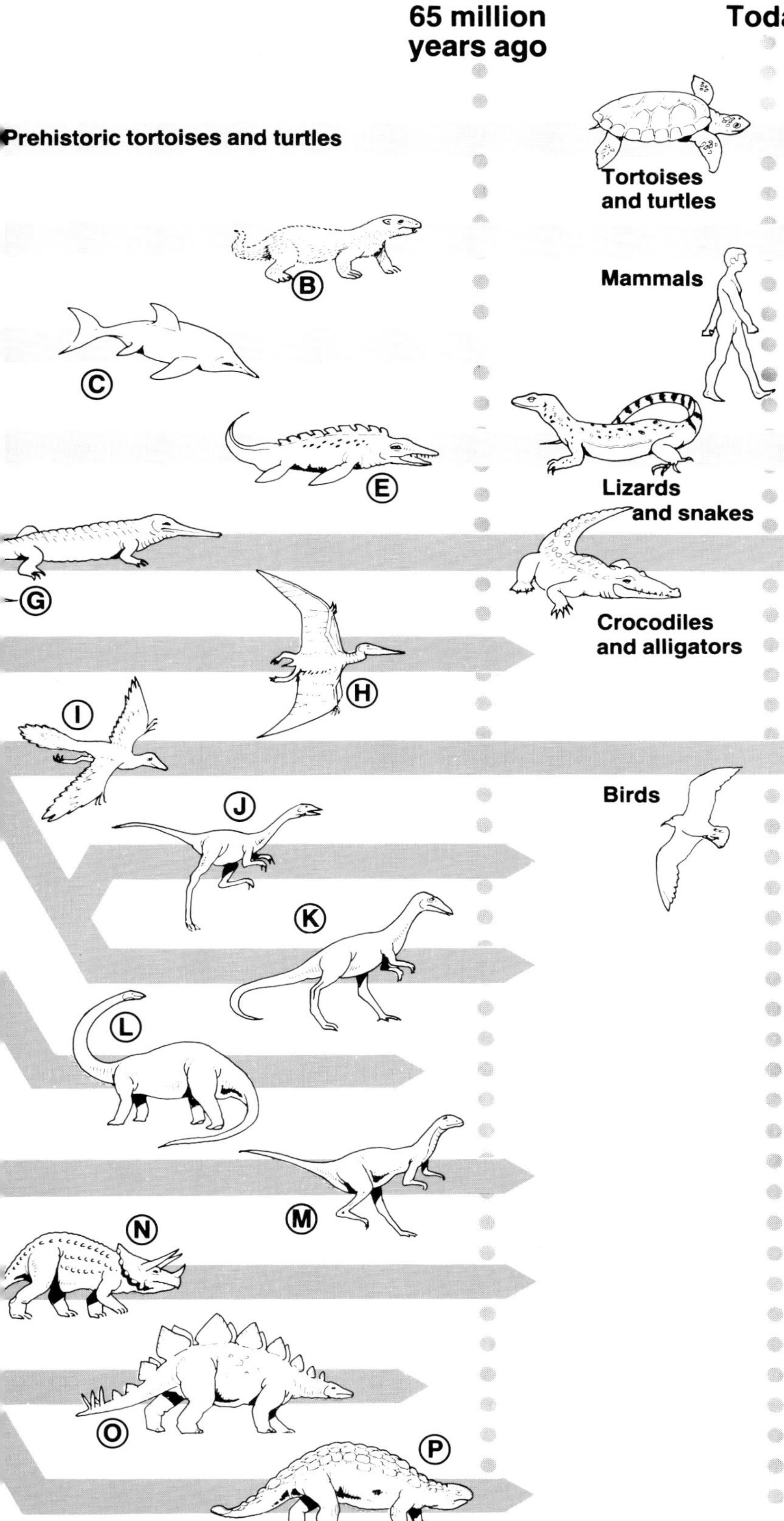

Ⓐ **Pelycosaurs** (mammal-like reptiles) were one of the first really successful reptile groups. Later they died out as the dinosaurs took over.

Ⓑ **Therapsids** were later mammal-like reptiles. When the dinosaurs disappeared the therapsids' mammalian descendants took over the world.

Ⓒ **Plesiosaurs and ichthyosaurs** were successful sea-going reptiles. Their line appeared about 200 million years ago, the placodonts being their early ancestors.

Ⓓ **Lepidosaurs** were prehistoric lizards, the distant ancestors of today's lizards and snakes. They evolved separately from the dinosaurs, about 250 million years ago. Lizards came first and snakes appeared about 100 million years ago.

Ⓔ **Mosasaurs** were large, fierce, sea-dwelling reptiles which had many similarities to lizards. Like other big reptiles they died out 65 million years ago.

Ⓕ **Thecodonts** were another group of 'stem reptiles'. In the beginning many were crocodile-like, but others soon evolved who were small and agile.

Ⓖ **Prehistoric crocodiles** first appeared about 200 million years ago. Some lived in the sea, others in fresh water. Crocodiles have remained much the same since.

Ⓗ **Pterosaurs** were flying reptiles that evolved some 200 million years ago. They developed long wings and a light body so that they resembled birds, but were in a separate group.

Ⓘ **Archaeopteryx** is the earliest bird yet discovered, from 147 million years ago. Birds probably evolved from the small meat-eating dinosaurs.

Ⓙ **'Ostrich dinosaurs'** were an offshoot of the meat-eating dinosaurs. They had toothless, beak-like jaws and the general shape of an ostrich with a long tail.

Ⓚ **Theropods** (meat-eating dinosaurs) stood on two legs, not four. They lived right through the Age of Dinosaurs and were very varied and successful.

Ⓛ **Sauropods** were the real giants – large, four-footed, plant-eating dinosaurs. The shape of their hips shows that they were probably related to meat-eating dinosaurs.

Ⓜ **Ornithopods** were two-legged herbivores. Some grew to a large size, others were small and fleet-footed. The 'duck-billed' dinosaurs were in this group.

Ⓝ **Ceratopsians** were horned dinosaurs with parrot-like beaks. They were successful towards the end of the Age of the Dinosaurs. Many were four-footed.

Ⓞ **Stegosaurs** were mostly large and four-footed. They appeared about 150 million years ago but became less common towards the end of the Age of Dinosaurs.

Ⓟ **Ankylosaurs** were medium-sized, four-footed dinosaurs with rather short legs. Their armour consisted of large bony plates in the skin.

How to say...

Lystrosaurus
Liss-trow-sore-us

Euparkeria
Ewe-parker-ear

Coelophysis
See-loff-eye-sis

Paradepedon
Para-dep-ee-don

Diplodocus
Dip-plod-owe-cuss

From field to laboratory

Fossils are found in all sorts of places, from seashores to high up in the mountains and from busy quarries to uninhabited deserts. The fossil expert has several tasks to carry out, once a fossil has been found. It must be carefully dug out of the rock, taken to the laboratory, cleaned up, repaired, and then studied. Some fossils are then exhibited to the public in museums.

Sometimes a mineralized fossil is harder than the surrounding rock. The fossil is left sticking out of its rock and it may sometimes be possible to pick up a whole fossil bone which is just lying on the ground.

Usually fossils are firmly embedded in the rock and have to be dug out. An embedded fossil is chipped free of as much rock as possible where it lies, so that it is easier to carry away. However, many fossils are too weak and fragile to dig out completely where they are found. In this case, a strengthening 'carrying case' is made around the fossils by coating them with plaster of Paris or a special hard-setting plastic foam before they are cut out.

In the laboratory the fossil is cut out of its man-made jacket, and then the rest of the rock is removed. In the old days a scientist had to chip away at the rock for hours on end with a hammer and chisel. This method is still used on tough specimens but there are now other ways of cleaning, as you can see on the right. The next thing to do is repair the fossil. A fossil bone may be in several pieces which need to be carefully glued together. Fossil skeletons often have parts of bones missing, but a skilled palaeontologist can reconstruct them.

Recovering fossils

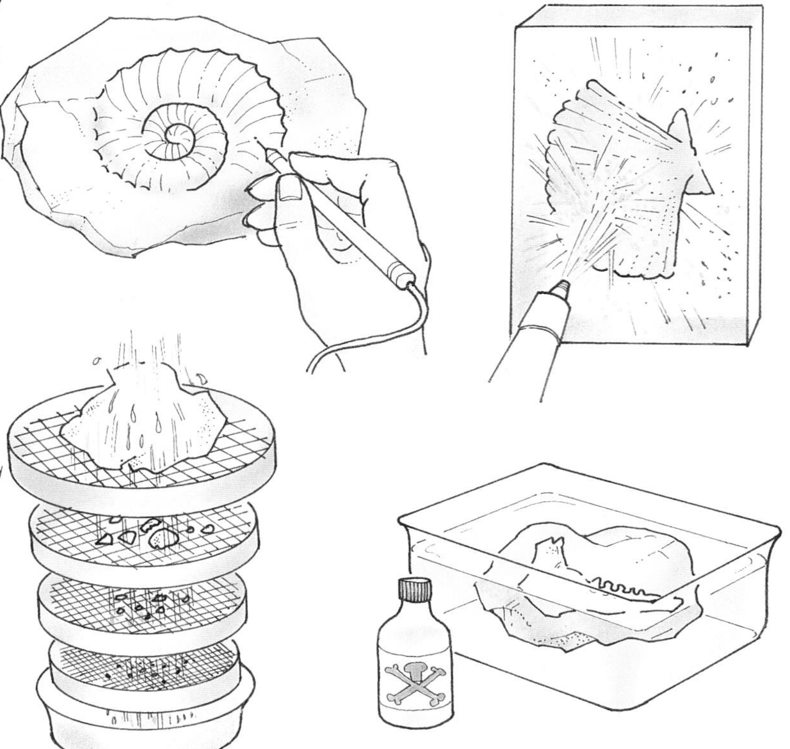

Picking and drilling
Some fossil specimens are worked on with small high-powered drills, sanders and picks – rather similar to the tools used by dentists! The operator often watches his work through a magnifying lens or microscope.

Sandblasting
If a small fossil is harder than the rock, it may be suitable for sandblasting. It is put in a small chamber and then grit or powder is blown at it under high pressure, which wears away the rock and leaves the fossil exposed.

Washing down
This method works on small fossils embedded in a rock – like chalk – that dissolves easily in water. The rock is put on the top of a tower of sieves, with the finest-mesh sieve at the base and the biggest-mesh one at the top. Water is then washed over the rock, which dissolves, and small fossils drop through the sieves.

Acid bathing
This is only used on fossils embedded in some types of limestone, which can be dissolved away by acid much more quickly than the fossil. The specimen is given repeated dips in baths of different acids. In between dips, the acid is washed off and exposed parts of the fossil are painted with an acid resistant coating to protect them.

Discovery to display
1. *Palaeontologists discover and start to dig out fossil bones.*
2. *The fossils are set in plaster to protect them when they are carried.*
3. *One part of the find – a skull – is prepared for display in a laboratory.*
4. *The reconstruction is complete, and the whole fossil skeleton is displayed in a museum.*

THE DINOSAURS ARRIVE

By the Jurassic period, from 195 to 136 million years ago, the dinosaurs had truly arrived. Species of all shapes and sizes dominated the land.

One of the smallest dinosaurs, *Compsognathus*, lived in the Jurassic. It was a swift hunter the size of a chicken. The biggest dinosaurs, the giant sauropods, also lived in this period. They walked on all fours and had long necks and small heads. The giant among these giants was *Brachiosaurus*, which grew up to 12 metres tall and weighed 75 tonnes – far bigger than any land animal before or since. It would have been about the height of seven tall men standing on each other's shoulders!

As well as the big sauropods there were many other plant-eaters, often heavily armoured with rows of plates or spines down their backs. In addition there were huge meat-eaters – taller than a house – which could tackle their big prey.

There were no dinosaurs in the water but plenty of other reptiles lived there. Ichthyosaurs and plesiosaurs (page 25) chased their prey through the seas, while prehistoric crocodiles snapped up fish in rivers and lakes.

There are plenty of sea fossils from the first part of the Jurassic, but few fossils of land-dwelling creatures exist. However, the land animals of the later Jurassic are well known from fossils found in America and East Africa. Their remains give us a good idea of what the world was like during the Age of Dinosaurs.

How to say...

Compsognathus
Comp-sog-nay-thuss

Apatosaurus
Ap-at-owe-sore-us

Camptosaurus
Camp-tow-sore-us

Archaeopteryx
Ark-ee-op-ter-icks

Stenosaurus
Sten-owe-sore-us

The plant eaters

Dinosaurs found fossilized with their food inside them are very rare indeed. So the lifestyles of these animals and what they ate have to be deduced from tell-tale clues, such as the size and shape of their teeth, jaws, heads and bodies.

Most plant food is not very nourishing, and many plants are rather tough. This means plant-eaters (called *herbivores)* must eat large quantities in order to get enough nourishment. They also need large stomachs and intestines to help mash and digest the food. It's useful to have teeth and jaws that can cut or grind the plant food into small pieces, too. There is generally no need for a plant-eater to be very speedy, since plants don't run away! However it might be useful for a small plant-eater to be able to outrun a predator.

Working from these clues, we might expect a plant-eating dinosaur to be large-bodied, not particularly quick, and with a head and jaws adapted to gathering and eating plants.

The biggest of all dinosaur bodies belonged to the sauropods like *Diplodocus* and *Brachiosaurus*. These massive bodies could obviously hold plenty of food. But what about the 'gathering end'? Most sauropods had small heads compared to their body size. Their jaws were not very powerful either and their

Long body
Diplodocus, *a sauropod, had a tiny head but a huge body. It must have spent nearly all its time eating. One skeleton measures nearly 27 metres long – the longest dinosaur yet discovered.*

Dawn at a riverbank during the Jurassic

1 Compsognathus *lived about 140 million years ago. It snatched at its prey of small animals with its hands.*

2 Apatosaurus, *otherwise known as* Brontosaurus, *had a giraffe-like neck which suggests that it browsed on leaves high in trees.*

3 Camptosaurus *(4 metres long) was a 'hoofed dinosaur' and so probably walked on all fours.*

4 Archaeopteryx *(40 cms long) is a famous fossil. Often called the first bird, some scientists nowadays call it a 'feathered dinosaur'.*

5 Stenosaurus, *6 metres in length, lived in rivers and seas along with other giant crocodiles.*

Armoured plant-eaters
Triceratops *(left) had huge rows of teeth. This dinosaur may have chopped up palm fronds with its jaws to feed on the sap.*
Stegosaurus *(right) had jaws shaped like a beak and small leaf-like teeth to shred juicy plants. It probably fed on fairly soft, low-growing vegetation.*

teeth were rather feeble little pegs. Obviously these dinosaurs could not chew up tough plant food, so how could they deal with it?

The answer to this seems to be that some sauropods had gizzards, as birds do. The gizzard is like a 'pre-stomach'. It's a muscular bag into which swallowed food passes. It squeezes and squashes the food against hard things like pebbles or pieces of grit that the sauropod has also swallowed. Sauropod skeletons have been found with polished pebbles inside or close by. These pebbles may well have been swallowed by the dinosaur, to be churned around with the plant food. So from this we can guess that sauropods did indeed have gizzards, because the pebbles would have become polished as they ground up the food.

All those teeth!

Hadrosaurs like *Anatosaurus* lived towards the end of the Age of Dinosaurs, when many of the world's plants were similar to those of today. *Anatosaurus* seems to have fed on some of the toughest kinds of woody plant food. We know this because the *mummified* (dried-out) remains of one of these dinosaurs has been found with twigs, seeds and conifer needles in its stomach.

To cope with this diet the hadrosaur had amazing rows of teeth along the sides of its mouth. These teeth never stopped growing and being replaced (like those of most reptiles). *Anatosaurus* could have had 2,000 teeth in its mouth at the same time!

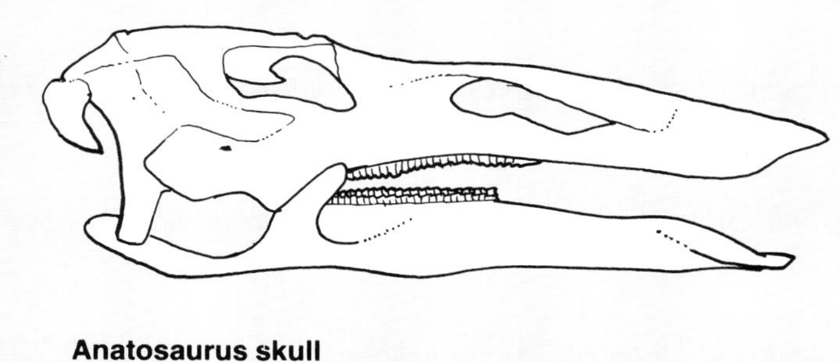

Anatosaurus skull

Dinosaur for dinner

Meat is a concentrated, nutritious food. Meat-eaters (called *carnivores*) generally don't need to consume huge quantities, and if they do have a large meal it may be some time before they need to eat again. So the body and intestines of a carnivore don't have to be especially big.

What a meat-eater does need, however, is the equipment to catch and cut up its prey. Many meat-eaters have good eyesight or a sensitive nose to help them find and track their meal. Their brains may well be quite large since they need flexible or 'intelligent' behaviour when hunting. Claws and teeth are usually big and sharp. Speed or agility may be necessary. The carnivorous dinosaurs showed many of these adaptations to the hunting way of life.

The 'tigers' of the dinosaur world were animals like *Allosaurus* – although at 12 metres long, this hunter was many times bigger than any tiger! Fossils show that its skull was light but large, 90 cms in length, and armed with ferocious, dagger-shaped teeth. These teeth had serrated edges, like saws. This creature's front and back feet had large, sharp claws. A predator like this would have been able to pounce and hold down its food with its claws, while at the same time slicing lumps of flesh with its teeth.

We do not know for certain what kind of prey *Allosaurus* took. It lived at the same time as huge sauropods such as *Diplodocus* and armoured dinosaurs

A fearsome foe
Allosaurus *lived about 150 million years ago. It used its long, heavy tail as a counterbalance as it strode along on two legs.*

The curse of the claw!

Deinonychus was a carnivorous dinosaur about 2 metres tall, and is shown on page 28. Here you can see the actual size of the claw on its second toe. The claw could be held up off the ground when *Deinonychus* ran along, to keep it sharp.

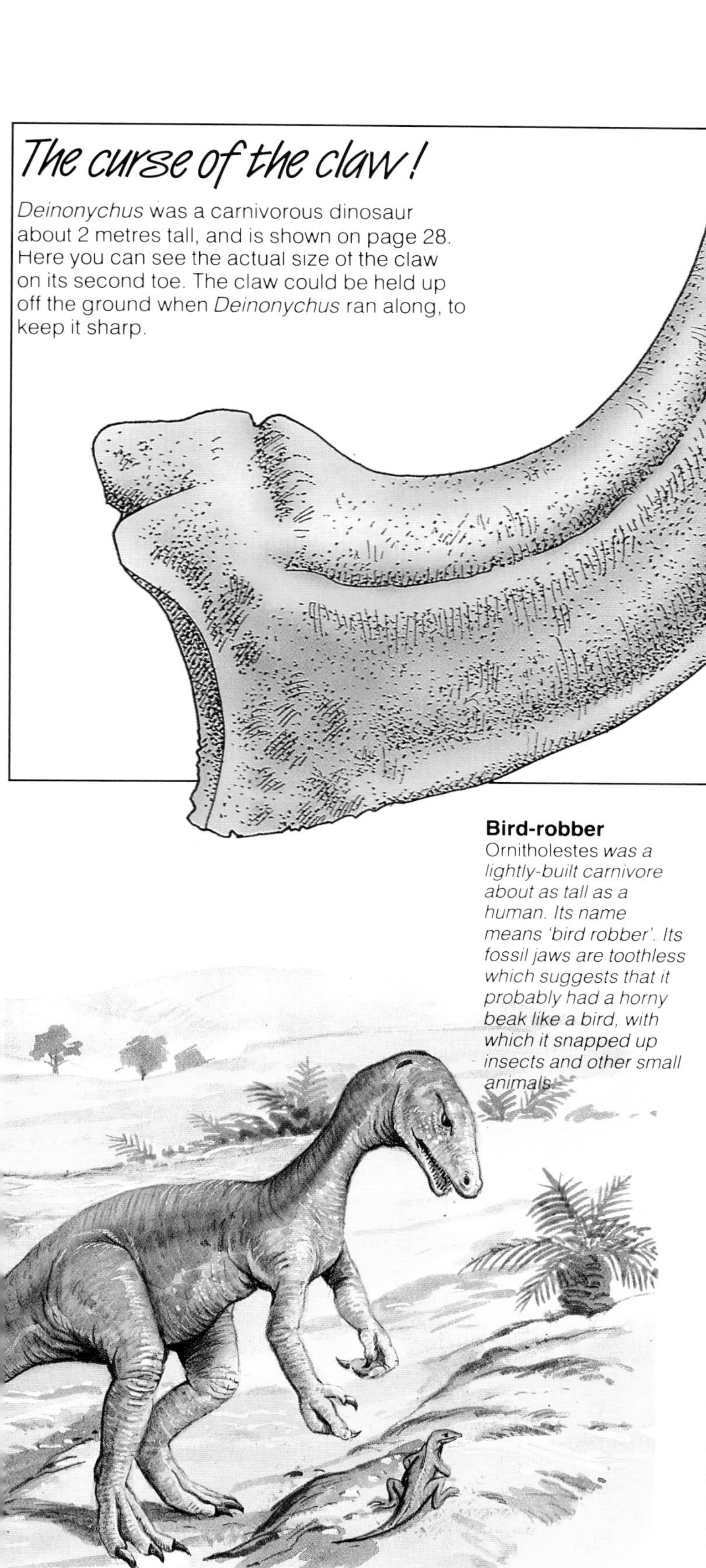

Bird-robber
Ornitholestes *was a lightly-built carnivore about as tall as a human. Its name means 'bird robber'. Its fossil jaws are toothless which suggests that it probably had a horny beak like a bird, with which it snapped up insects and other small animals.*

like *Stegosaurus*, so these may have been its prey. But like modern-day hunters it's likely that *Allosaurus* took whatever it could surprise.

The biggest carnivore of all time was *Tyrannosaurus*. It lived towards the end of the Age of Dinosaurs. This huge hunter was 12 metres long, 5 metres high and may have weighed around 7 tonnes. Its skull and jaws were very strongly built, possibly to cope with the struggles of its prey.

Tyrannosaurus used to be thought of as a slow-moving carrion feeder – meaning that it picked on dead and dying food. But its body shape and its skull and teeth tell us that it was an active animal. Fossils of its 'hands' have not been found, so these are usually reconstructed like its relation *Albertosaurus* which had two tiny fingers. What this huge, powerful dinosaur used its tiny arms for is still a puzzle. They were so short they couldn't even reach its mouth!

Discovering dinosaurs

People have been finding fossil dinosaur bones for many hundreds of years. But a long time ago no one knew what they were. Some people thought they were the bones of human giants. It was only about 160 years ago that people began to realise that these were the remains of giant, extinct reptiles.

In 1822 Gideon Mantell worked as a doctor in Sussex, in southern England. His hobby was geology (studying rocks). Apparently, one day his wife, while waiting for him to finish visiting a patient, discovered some large teeth in a heap of gravel at the roadside. Mantell traced the gravel to a certain quarry and there he found more fragments. But the teeth were unlike anything he had seen before. Even experts were no help. They assumed that the teeth belonged to a rhino or other large mammal.

At last Mantell met someone who had seen similar teeth, but much smaller, which belonged to the South American lizard *Iguana*. Mantell's idea that the fossil teeth were from a reptile seemed to be true. He invented the name *Iguanodon* ('iguana tooth') for their owner, who he thought was a giant lizard.

In 1824 another geologist, William Buckland, examined some fossil fragments including a jaw with teeth. He suspected they came from a huge meat-eating fossil reptile which he called *Megalosaurus*. Neither Buckland nor Mantell would have called these animals dinosaurs, as the word was not invented until 1841 (see page 12).

In 1858 dinosaur fossils were discovered in the United States. They were part of a *Hadrosaurus* skeleton.

Joseph Leidy made the first accurate reconstruction of a dinosaur. Soon after, people were able to make sense of the 'giant bird' tracks that had been found in Massachusetts as long ago as 1802. They were in fact dinosaur footprints.

A huge number of dinosaur discoveries were made in North America in the later part of the nineteenth century. This was partly due to the rivalry between two fossil collectors, Edward Cope and Charles Marsh. In 20 years from about 1870 to 1890 they found over 130 new kinds of dinosaur. Soon dinosaur fossils were found in other countries. *Brachiosaurus* was discovered in Tanzania, and dinosaur eggs were uncovered in Mongolia (page 30). Dinosaur fossils have now been found almost all over the world.

The best known dinosaur

Iguanodon, besides being one of the first dinosaurs ever discovered, is also very famous. In 1878 a huge collection of fossil *Iguanodon* skeletons was found in a mine in Belgium. The scene at the discovery must have looked like that shown in the old print on the left. Scientists spent years studying the bones – as did many other interested museum visitors (below, left). Now we know this ornithopod dinosaur better than almost any other. It lived about 115 million years ago and grew up to 9 metres long. *Iguanodon* (shown alive, below) probably ate plants, which it cut off with the hard, beak-like front of its mouth. It then crushed the food with the grinding teeth at the back of its mouth.

REPTILES OF THE SEAS

During the time that the dinosaurs ruled the land, other reptiles took over the seas. One group that flourished briefly in the Triassic period were the placodonts. They had flat teeth for crushing shellfish and some were armour-plated like turtles. Fossils of the first true turtles have been found dating from the Triassic. By the end of the Age of Dinosaurs, turtles were similar to today's – but much bigger, with some growing to be over 4 metres long.

Ichthyosaurs were common sea-dwelling reptiles in the Jurassic period. Their name means 'fish-lizards' and they had a fish-like fin in the middle of their backs and a large tail to thrust them through the water. Their limbs had evolved into steering paddles. Plesiosaurs were another group of marine reptiles that lived in the Jurassic seas. They had large paddle-shaped limbs which they used to row themselves through the water. *Mosasaurus* was yet another giant sea reptile, from the late Cretaceous. This was a huge relation of today's monitor lizard and had ferocious rows of sharp teeth.

Not all the creatures shown here lived at the same time. Nevertheless, during the Age of Reptiles few sea creatures were safe from these predatory marine reptiles. But it was all to no avail. When the end came for the land dinosaurs and their flying cousins, the sea reptiles went with them.

How to say...

Archelon
Ark-ay-lon

Placodus
Plack-owe-dus

Henodus
Hen-owe-dus

Ichthyosaurus
Ikth-ee-owe-sore-us

Cryptoclidus
Crip-tow-clide-us

Success or failure?

People often use the word dinosaur to mean something which is big, old and a failure! But were the dinosaurs really failures?

In the sense that they became extinct, while other creatures like the mammals survived, they did fail. However this may have been due to some very unusual changes in the world around them. If such drastic changes happened today, many mammals would die out.

It is impossible to say what might have happened had the dinosaurs lived on. We do know that, right up to the time of their extinction 65 million years ago, they still seemed to be successful. They dominated the land and were still evolving into new and improved forms, right to their sudden end.

Dinosaurs have sometimes been called stupid or slow-witted. Some perhaps were. *Stegosaurus*, for example, had an amazingly small brain for its size. Its brain was only 3 cms long while the body was 6 metres long! But many of the other dinosaurs, as far as fossils tell us, did not have especially small brains. In fact some of the small meat-eaters like *Stenonychosaurus* had large brains and may have been quite intelligent.

There is much argument about whether dinosaurs were cold-blooded, like today's reptiles, or warm-blooded, that is able to keep their bodies at a constant temperature, like birds and mammals. The inside of some fossil dinosaur bones looks like the inside of mammal bones, which some scientists

Mammal ancestor
Megazostrodon *fossils have been found in southern Africa. This early mammal lived at a time when the dinosaurs were only just beginning their reign.*

Brains, not brawn
Stenonychosaurus *lived about 80 million years ago. Its large head contained a big brain in proportion to its body, which was only 1 ½ metres long. It may well have been a fairly clever hunter, tricking or trapping its prey.*

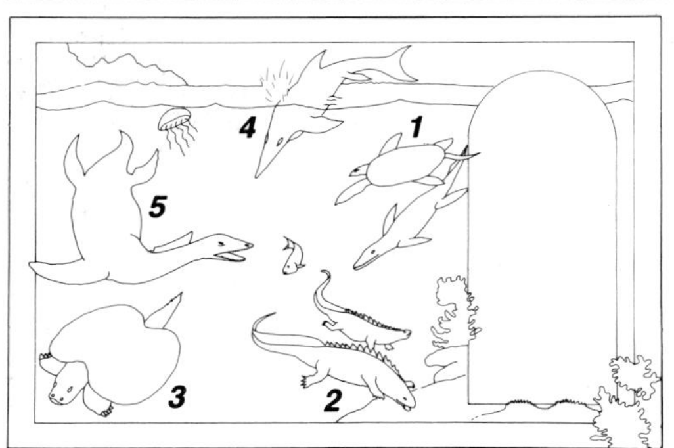

Ocean dwellers of the Age of Reptiles

1 Archelon *was up to 4 metres long and weighed 3 tonnes, making it the largest turtle known.*

2 Placodus *lived in shallow seas and on the shores. It grew to over 2 metres long and fed on shellfish.*

3 Henodus *(1 metre long), a placodont, is from Triassic seas. It resembled a turtle but it was not a close relative.*

4 Ichthyosaurus *was one of the best-known 'fish-lizards' and was about 3 metres long. It hunted in groups, preying mainly on belemnites whose shells are preserved inside some fossil ichthyosaurs.*

5 Cryptoclidus *3 metres long, was a plesiosaur. Some people who believe in the 'Loch Ness Monster' think it may be a plesiosaur just like this one!*

Dinosaur look-alikes

Some dinosaurs were very similar in body size and shape to animals in the world today. For example, with its long thin neck and legs, *Hypsilophodon* had similarities with an antelope, while *Palaeoscinus* resembled an armadillo. These resemblances were due to them evolving in similar surroundings and leading similar ways of life to their look-alikes today. Similarities like these are called *evolutionary convergence*.

say is evidence for their warm-bloodedness. Other scientists say that a large dinosaur in what we think was a warm climate would be warm most of the time anyway. For the time being the arguments go on and no one can say for sure.

But in one respect, as far as we know, all dinosaurs were 'primitive'. They laid eggs. They did not give birth to live young, like most mammals. Neither did they have certain physical and behavioural 'improvements' that went with giving birth. In this respect the dinosaurs fell behind the reptiles' other evolutionary line, the therapsids (page 13).

DINOSAUR HEYDAY

The heyday of the dinosaurs was during the Cretaceous period, from 136 to 65 million years ago. Dinosaurs covered the land in greater variety and with more advanced designs than ever before. The big four-footed sauropods still walked the Earth, but as time went by they began to die out and new types of plant-eaters took their place. *Iguanodon* was one of these.

At the beginning of the Cretaceous the warm, wet landscape was very different to the one we know today. Large plants such as seed-ferns and cycads had been around for a long time, but new types of plant were slowly taking over. These were flowers and trees – familiar to us today. Grasses, however, had not yet evolved and so there were no wide, open, grassy plains.

By the end of the Cretaceous many recognisable plants and animals were living on the Earth. Oak and magnolia trees were common, ducks and herons lived on the lakes and rivers. The dinosaurs were adapting well, and near the end of the Cretaceous there was a huge array of species. Plant-eaters included the duck-bills, four-legged armoured dinosaurs and horned dinosaurs. These herbivores provided food for many meat-eaters such as the largest carnivore ever to walk the land – the Cretaceous dinosaur *Tyrannosaurus*. Who would have guessed that within a few million years every single dinosaur, and most other large reptiles, would have gone forever?

How to say...

Corythosaurus
Corry-thow-sore-us

Tyrannosaurus
Ty-ran-owe-sore-us

Styracosaurus
Sty-rack-owe-sore-us

Deinonychus
Day-non-ee-cus

Ornithomimus
Ore-nith-owe-mime-us

Triceratops
Try-cerra-tops

We can only guess the answers to many of the questions we have about how dinosaurs lived. Did they live in groups? Did they look after their young? Did males and females look different? How did they breed? We will probably never know the truth about most dinosaurs. Just occasionally, though, fossils give us a fascinating glimpse into the past and we can answer some of these questions for a particular kind of dinosaur.

Hollow nests

Fossil nests of the small dinosaur *Protoceratops* have been found in Mongolia. These nests were hollows that the dinosaur dug in the sand. Inside the nests were about 12 eggs, which were arranged in a kind of spiral, as they were laid. Fossils of this dinosaur have been discovered in various stages of growth, from hatchling to adult. We now know how *Protoceratops* changed in size and shape as it grew.

An American/Asian scene during the Cretaceous

1 Corythosaurus, *which grew to 13 metres in length, was a 'duck-billed' dinosaur.*

2 Tyrannosaurus, *the largest meat-eater ever, had dagger-like teeth up to 15 cms long, with which it killed and slashed at its prey.*

3 Styracosaurus *(5 metres long) had an impenetrable array of horns on its armour-plated head. It ate plants.*

4 Deinonychus *stood just taller than a human. It probably used the ferocious claws on its second toes to slash at its prey.*

5 Ornithomimus *was one of the 'ostrich dinosaurs'.*

6 Triceratops *was one of the last dinosaurs. They were alive up to the point of the great extinction, 65 million years ago.*

Herds and tracks

Sometimes many dinosaurs of one type are found together. This can lead scientists to deduce that they were a herd struck down by tragedy. On the other hand such 'herds' may be bones that collected over a period of time, perhaps washed together each year by a flood.

Tracks showing 20 or more dinosaurs all moving through the same area, in the same direction, are good evidence of herds. *Iguanodon* tracks, shown here, indicate several animals apparently moving together. From what we know of large plant-eating animals today, like zebras or antelopes, it would seem very likely that some herbivorous dinosaurs did live in groups. This would give them some protection from large meat-eaters.

Mums and dads

Did male and female dinosaurs look different? From what we know of present-day reptiles, the answer is probably yes. It is difficult to spot the difference in fossils, but it is sometimes possible. Two types of Iguanodon *have been found in Europe. One was larger and more heavily built than the other. They could be different species, but some scientists think that they were males and females of the same species.*

Nesting like birds?

Perhaps the most interesting fossil nest found belongs to the hadrosaur *Maiasaurus*. These dinosaurs made nests with a mud rim and, after hatching, the young seem to have stayed in the nest for a while. We know this because in addition to hatchling-sized young, remains of other, larger youngsters have been found in fossil nests. These had worn teeth, which would seem to show that the young were fed in the nest by their parents, as birds do today.

The reptiles take off

Several different kinds of reptile have taken to the air. The modern 'flying dragon' lizard glides from tree to tree on 'wings' of stretched skin. Over 200 million years ago *Kuhneosaurus* was gliding and it had better wings than its modern relation. But gliding like this is not true flying, it's only an addition to a mainly earthbound life. The reptiles which really mastered the air – other than those that evolved into birds – were the pterosaurs.

Pterosaurs, like dinosaurs, evolved from a group of lightly-built archosaurs (page 11). In some ways their bodies became very similar to those of birds, but pterosaurs had developed quite separately.

Giant scavenger?
In 1972 the remains of huge Quetzalcoatlus, *were discovered. They are not complete, but they indicate a creature like* Pteranodon *– yet much larger, with a wingspan of 15 metres! This monster seems to have lived over land, not sea, and may have scavenged like a modern vulture.*

In pterosaurs, the front limbs became wings. The arm and hand stayed much the same as in other reptiles, but the main difference was in the fingers. Three of these stuck out at the front, while the fourth finger was the extraordinary one. Each of its bones became enormously long, to support the wing itself. The wing was made of leathery skin, not feathers, and its outline can be seen clearly in some fossils.

Many old pictures of what scientists thought pterosaurs looked like, show the wing attached to the hind limb. However this is no longer certain. Also, pterosaurs used to be thought of only as gliders, swooping above the sea in which they fished, then returning to cliffs or islands to roost. Scientists used to think that a pterosaur's muscles were not strong enough for flapping, that the creature was too clumsy to move on land, and that it could only take off by jumping from a tree or cliff.

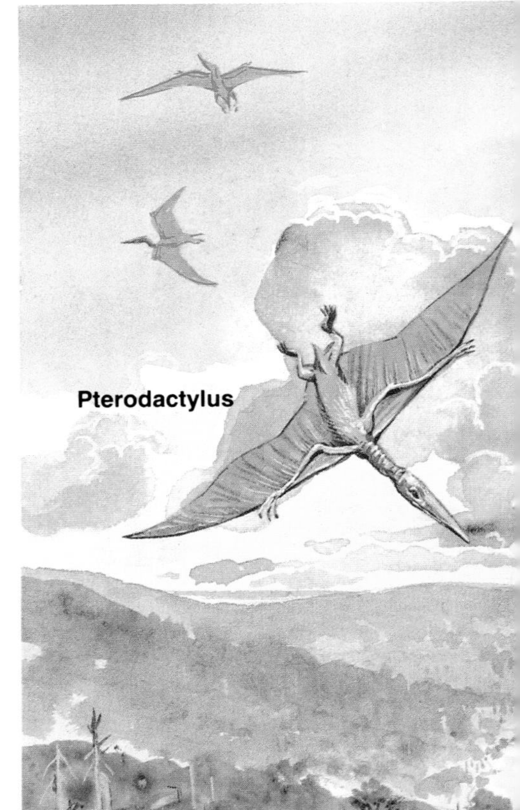

But as pterosaurs are studied more closely and more fossil discoveries are made, it now seems quite likely that none of these things are true. Pterosaurs may have been just as good at flying as birds. Being active, flying creatures they might even have been warm-blooded. Several scientists suggested that pterosaurs may have had fur, to keep themselves warm, and some experts thought they could see traces of hair on fossils. In 1970 a Russian scientist discovered remains of the pterosaur *Sordes* with what looked very much like a furry covering.

All sizes of pterosaur

Some pterosaurs were very small. Pterodactylus *of 150 million years ago was only the size of a starling. It may have caught insects with its small teeth while flying.*

Others were bigger. Rhamphorhynchus *from 140 million years ago had a wingspan of 1 ½ metres. Its long tail probably helped to balance it and acted as a rudder as it changed direction in mid-air. It had pointed teetn and may have been a fish-eater.*

Some pterosaurs, like the giant Pteranodon *that lived 80 million years ago, were toothless. It had a wingspan of over 7 metres and may well have been the pterosaur equivalent of the albatross, spending long periods gliding effortlessly over the ocean.*

Fitted out for flying

Many parts of a pterosaur's body were designed for flight, just like a bird of today. Can you see any other similarities between pterosaurs and birds?

Large brain, with the parts dealing with sight and balance especially big.

Light bones with air holes in them to reduce weight.

Hairy body to keep heat in, allowing the pterosaur to stay active in cold weather.

In some pterosaurs the legs were like those of a small dinosaur. Such peterosaurs could probably walk and perhaps even run.

Large, flat breastbone to anchor the powerful muscles that flapped the wings.

Helmets, spines & armour

Large slow-moving animals need protection against predators. For many dinosaurs this protection took the form of some sort of armour-plating. Fossilized dinosaur skin has been found with large, tough scales in it. The same type of tough skin with bony plates in it can be seen in the dinosaurs' present-day relatives, the crocodiles. But in some dinosaurs the protective armour was much more elaborate.

In the ankylosaur group of dinosaurs, like *Euoplocephalus*, the whole back was armoured with strong knobs of bone set into the skin. Strong bony plates covered the head and spines stuck out from the neck and shoulders. Smaller spines went down the back to the base of the tail. The tail itself had large, strong bones and on its end was a huge club made of plates of bone welded together in the skin. This dinosaur tail would have been a very powerful weapon when swung against any hungry meat-eaters.

The slow-moving *Stegosaurus* also had armour. This was made up of bony plates along its back. The plates were apparently arranged alternately, starting with small ones behind the head and increasing in size to the hip and base of the tail. The end of the tail had spines. A few scientists have suggested that these bony plates lay flat on the dinosaur's back, but most believe they were upright.

In the upright position the plates could have had another use besides protection. Skin-covered plates of this size and position could have helped to absorb heat when cold or lose it when hot (like the *Dimetrodons's* sail shown on page 5). The fossilized bony plates have many little grooves in them, which could have had small blood vessels running through them. This would increase the efficiency of the plates as coolers or warmers.

Plated for protection
The ankylosaur Euoplocephalus *was so well armoured that it even had hard, bony plates in its eyelids!*

The call of the wild

Some of the 'duck-billed' dinosaurs had crests on their heads. But fossils show that the crest was not solid bone. It was hollow, usually with air passages from the nostrils to the throat passing through it. Perhaps it was used as a vibrating or resonating chamber, to make the dinosaur's calls louder. Modern alligators make extremely loud booming calls at mating time. So prehistoric reptiles may well have done the same. A dinosaur like *Parasaurolophus* which was 10 metres long, had a crest 1 metre long. If this resonated when the dinosaur made its call, the sound could have been heard miles away!

Head-banging

The male Stegoceras *may have used its thick, strong head to butt rival males at breeding time, as in the picture below. The winner of the competition would get to mate with the females. This dinosaur belonged to a group called the 'dome-heads'.*

Keeping it cool

The plates along the back of Stegosaurus *could have helped control body temperature as well as acting as protection.*

The changing world of the dinosaur

Animals and plants were not the only things to evolve and change during the Age of the Dinosaurs. The land under the dinosaurs' feet was itself changing and moving.

We tend to think of the Earth and its continents as being fixed. In fact the continents are gradually creeping across the Earth's surface, to take up new positions.

They have been on the move since well before the time of the dinosaurs. When dinosaurs first appeared the landmasses of the Earth had all come together in a 'supercontinent' that scientists have called Pangaea. Over millions of years this split up and the pieces moved into the positions familiar to us from maps and photographs today.

The idea of 'continental drift' was first suggested in 1915 by Alfred Wegener, who noticed the jigsaw fit between the continents in their outlines and rock formations. At this time his ideas were rejected but today they are assumed to be true. Scientists have only recently been able to carry out research and make measurements to explain how the continents move.

Alfred Wegener
German explorer and geology theorist, Wegener first put forward the idea of 'continental drift' in 1915.

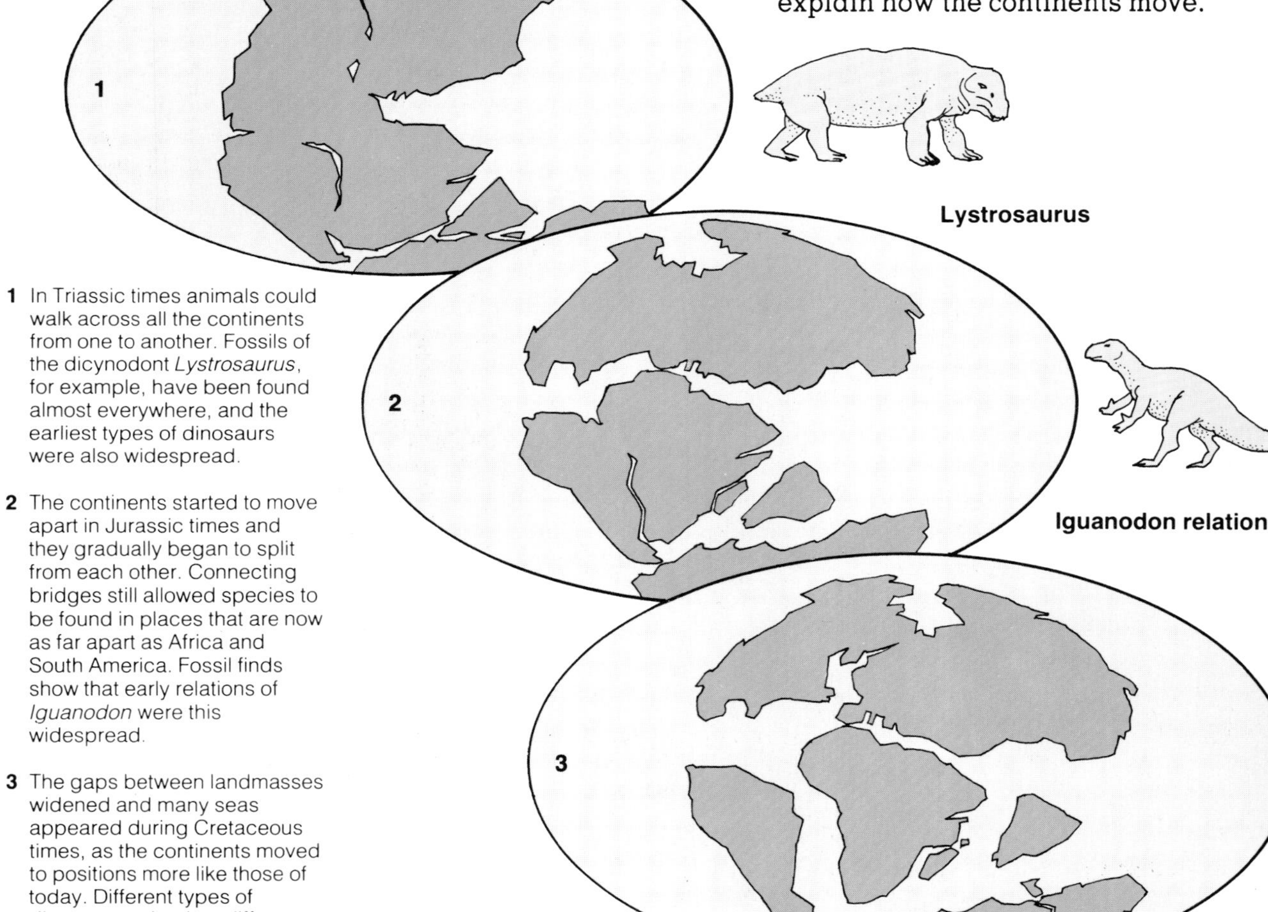

1 In Triassic times animals could walk across all the continents from one to another. Fossils of the dicynodont *Lystrosaurus*, for example, have been found almost everywhere, and the earliest types of dinosaurs were also widespread.

2 The continents started to move apart in Jurassic times and they gradually began to split from each other. Connecting bridges still allowed species to be found in places that are now as far apart as Africa and South America. Fossil finds show that early relations of *Iguanodon* were this widespread.

3 The gaps between landmasses widened and many seas appeared during Cretaceous times, as the continents moved to positions more like those of today. Different types of dinosaur evolved on different landmasses – until the mysterious catastrophe that made them all extinct.

INDEX